ESTABLISHING A STRUCTURED ORGANISATION:

CULTURE OF EXCELLENCE FOR LEADERSHIP

James T. Mayberry

All rights reserved. No part of this publication may be reproduced, distributed, or transmitted in any form or by any means, including photocopying, recording, or other electronic or mechanical methods, without the prior written permission of the publisher, except in the case of brief quotations embodied in critical reviews and certain other noncommercial uses permitted by copyright law.

Copyright © James T. Mayberry, 2022.

Table of contents

Introduction

Chapter 1 **What Is a Culture Of Excellence?**

Chapter 2 **How Is Culture Related to Performance and Results?**

Chapter 3 **Why Is Skills Development Training Not Enough?**

Chapter 4 **Why is leadership coaching not enough?**

Chapter 5 **How Does Powerful Organisational Change Begin?**

Chapter 6 **Three Steps to Building a Sustainable High Performance Organisation**

   a. *Culture and mindset: the key ingredient for success*
   b. *Skills training*
   c. *Coaching: How to make your development programs stick*

Chapter 7 **Building a Culture of Excellence Organisation- Wide**

   a. *Leadership Excellence*
   b. *Sales Excellence*

c. Customer service Excellence
d. Team Excellence
e. Operational Excellence

Chapter 8 **Sustaining Excellence: Don't Settle for Short-Term Results**

Chapter 9 **Does Your Company Need a Corporate Culture Health Check?**

Chapter 10 **Understanding how Organised Structure Builds Culture Of Excellence**

Chapter 11 **How to Design Your Organisation's Structure**

Introduction

Leaders never aim for mediocrity. Do you agree? Who gets up in the morning and thinks, "let's have some average results today!". Not very likely. Leaders strive to harness full potential, chase hyper-growth, construct an effective organisation and make enduring change. The fact of the matter is that:

"Many leadership, corporate culture and training and development programs create just short-term advantages that slip away when teams go back to their old habits."

This means that the main task for any leadership team is to develop a lasting culture of excellence throughout the entire firm. The key to shifting your firm from the status quo to an expectation of excellence is your corporate culture. When you establish a culture of excellence, you create organisational capacity and a structure that empowers, concentrates and engages individuals.

"The key to transforming your organisation from the status quo to an expectation of excellence is your corporate culture."

Chapter 1

1. What Is a Culture of Excellence?
As a leader, you don't go to work every day expecting subpar outcomes. Nonetheless, your behaviour or concentration may be inadvertently creating mediocre expectations. Unfortunately, many organisational and commercial leaders fall into this trap.

Every leader and business owner desires instant results, improved performance, and long-term transformation. Many leadership, corporate culture, and training programs, on the other hand, offer only short-term advantages that vanish when teams revert to their old behaviours.

Moving your organisation from mediocrity to excellence necessitates a fundamental shift in corporate culture. When you establish an exceptional company culture, you build organisational capacity and a structure that empowers, focuses, and engages individuals. You cease squandering a lot of time and money cultivating an antiquated problem-solving culture. Instead, you provide your teams with the mentality and abilities they need to focus on achieving the intended objectives.

What are Key Characteristics of a Culture of Excellence?

1. *A Compelling Organisational Vision that is well Communicated and Understood*
It's not enough to simply have a stated organisational vision. To achieve a Culture of Excellence, every employee must understand not only the company's vision, but also know their own roles, responsibilities and the specific actions they need to take in order to help achieve this vision.

2. *Clear Purpose and Meaning*
In a Culture of Excellence, employees feel that what they are working on is meaningful, significant, and purpose-based. Everyone concerned is highly inspired by the common

purpose, which becomes the driving force behind everything that they do.

3. *Mastery of Roles and Focus on High Performers*

Most companies unconsciously concentrate on problem solving and fire fighting and end up rewarding mediocrity. In fact, many managers actually enable their low performers by focusing their time and energy on trying to solve their problems — while paying a disproportionate amount of time to their high performers. Those high performers eventually leave the organisation because they aren't being recognized or rewarded for their hard work.

Companies with a Culture of Excellence set an expectation of high performance organization-wide. Every employee is supported and encouraged to become a master in their role and area of expertise. High performers are nurtured, rewarded, mentored and recognized, and average performers are coached to move into the high performance category.

In these cultures, there is no place for low performers, and they either move up or leave the organisation.

4. *Resilience to Change and Challenges*
In most organisations, when change or challenges occur, employees become distracted and lose focus on the organisational vision and goals. In a Culture of Excellence, employees develop the flexibility and resilience to deal with change, challenge and uncertainty.

Even when there are obstacles and challenges that may seem impossible to overcome, the motivation to achieve the organisational vision is higher than the urge to avoid discomfort and pain. With that clarity of purpose and a strong desire to succeed, they push through the barriers and move forward toward their vision. Managers support their teams in staying focused and on track, despite difficulties and challenges.

5. *Highly Collaborative Teams*
Most of us have worked at companies where the silo mentality reigns. Teams and individuals closely guard their expertise, projects and knowledge. Collaboration across teams is nearly non-existent unless forced. A key feature of a Culture of Excellence is highly collaborative

teams—both internal and external. Because every employee and all teams are
working together toward a common organisational vision, they feel they are on the same side. And because this collaboration is encouraged and rewarded from the top down, there is no more reason to protect individual roles, projects or expertise.

6. *Pioneer Mentality*

Most companies that achieve a Culture of Excellence do not settle for mediocre. Instead,
They are focused on creating something that has never been created before, breaking records and achieving unprecedented results. From the outside, it may seem as if they are achieving the impossible. The resulting energy, excitement and drive creates a certain
positive tension that reverberates throughout the company. Employees and teams are
encouraged to explore, nurture and co-create to achieve common goals.

Chapter 2

2. How Is Culture Related to Performance and Results?

If your company were a computer, its operating system would be its corporate culture.

Otherwise, your software products will simply not work until you have the proper operating system installed. It's the same with your company. You will not reach your performance goals if you do not have the correct corporate culture in place, no matter how much time and money you invest.

Many CEOs believe that business culture is an intangible idea. When their firm faces obstacles, they resort to what they see as more solid remedies, such as team development or skill training. Unfortunately, these operations are analogous to putting out little bush fires without taking into account the current temperature or surroundings. They frequently address simply the symptoms rather than the underlying issue. In actuality, corporate culture is a quantifiable and measurable term. Working on your corporate culture allows you to address the root cause of any challenges you may be having while also gaining access to the solution to true growth and the business results you desire.

The Bottom Line Results You've Been Looking For

Because corporate culture deals with every aspect of your business, you can expect to see measurable improvements in productivity, revenue generation, retention of high performers, and alignment, and team collaboration

- Committed and engaged employees working toward common goals
- Loyalty and commitment to the vision and values of the organisation
- People who are happy and proud to be part of something 'Big' that they are
creating together
- More satisfied customers that keep on coming back
- Increased efficiencies and productivity
- Overall improvements in profitability and market share.

Companies with the strongest corporate cultures tend to be the companies you read about in the media. They are the market leaders and market shapers. They are constantly creating new products and, in some cases, inventing the future. They are innovative and constantly learning and tend to add significant value to society. These are companies creating break-throughs in fields such as medicine, technology, research, and communications.

Chapter 3

3. Why Is Skills Development Training Not Enough?

If your company is like most, you are unaware that the root cause of most of your organisational problems is an underdeveloped or poor corporate culture that is out of alignment with your strategy, so you waste valuable resources treating the symptoms, which usually take the form of better planning, team building activities, or implementing new processes or skill training. Problems in a group? Let's perform some team building activities outside. Concerns about leadership? Send the manager to leadership development classes. Team building and skill development will not address your corporate culture issue.Here's why.

Team Building Sessions:
Team building type activities like river rafting, bowling, skiing and weekends away are a lot of fun. But when your teams return from their fun activities, the same issues reappear within a few days or a week. This is because you're skating

around the real issues and dealing with symptoms.

Skills Development Training:
Sending people to skills development training in sales, leadership and service is a common initial response to problems in the organisation. However, when the culture is stifling, or not positive or constructive, people aren't engaged or interested. And when they're not interested, they don't care. So when you send employees to these training programs (that cost a lot of money) they are present because they have to be, but they don't take much in. And when they go back to work, they still aren't happy with their managers or they still have issues with team members because these core issues were never addressed.

The Connection Between Culture and Skills Training:
There is a direct correlation between the culture of the organisation and the skills and
behaviours of the people. Skills training and development programs are ineffective without a positive culture in place.When an organisation

has a constructive or positive culture, people are more receptive because they are more engaged. And when they are more receptive and engaged and are sent to learn new skills, they want to be there. As a result, their level of learning increases significantly and so does your return on investment. When they return from training, you see the results right away.The important thing to remember is that while technical and skills training are important, they should be seen as a second step to be taken only after a positive corporate culture has been established. Only this results in engaged employees who are ready to learn and to apply what they have learned to achieve their goals. If this culture is not yet in place,your training and development programs will simply never produce the results you would hope for.

Chapter 4

4. Why is leadership coaching not enough?

Many managers are promoted from within the corporation, and not elected as leaders by their teams. Furthermore, corporations tend to elevate the best operators to become managers and these operators may or may not have any experience or abilities in managing people and leading teams. To make up for this, they are sent to leadership skills training or coaching programs. However, when they are sent to leadership skills or coaching programs, these new managers typically don't utilise the lessons. They may try one or more of the skills when they get back to the office, but then they typically feel uncomfortable and stop and find excuses as to why the skills training didn't work. The difficulty is that these programs tend to focus on theories and broad abilities, but most of these tools are either not practical enough or are applied in the inappropriate context. And if the managers don't have the proper attitude in place, and the correct culture back in the business, they won't have the confidence or guts to deal with challenging problems or personalities. As a result, they avoid managing unpleasant situations—and do not employ the coaching and leadership abilities they were trained to use.

A Culture-First Approach to Leadership Coaching

In 2012, Forbes magazine posted an article declaring that, "Training is the #1 reason leadership development fails." Why is this so? Skills-based leadership programs are simply not enough. Your leadership team may lack confidence, willingness and focus. Additionally, they may not be engaged or may lack the motivation and drive to achieve your organisation's goals. In fact, a Towers Perrin Global Workforce study of 90,000 workers world-wide (including 5,000 in Canada) revealed that only 23% of employees consider themselves highly engaged. If your leaders and managers do not take full responsibility for their own performance and for that of their teams, and if they don't change their mindset and attitude, no amount of skills training will ever deliver results.

However, if you focus first on building the right leadership culture and mindset, confidence problems and fear of change will disappear, and your leadership team will be engaged and ready to learn and apply new tools, strategies, and tactics.

Chapter 5

5. How Does Powerful Organisational Change Begin?

Whether it's at work or in our day-to-day lives, the desire to avoid discomfort and uncertainty overrides nearly everything else. That is why effectively managing organisational change is a monumental challenge for most organisations.

While companies want their teams to be focused on organisational goals, employees are more motivated to avoid change, fear and uncertainty. In order to keep their teams focused, many companies resort to a problem-solving style of response. Unfortunately, it is exactly this style of response that backfires and moves companies even further away from their intended results.

Reaction and Problem Solving Is Not the Right Strategy for Change

When companies spend their time and energy focusing on getting people back on track, they automatically become reactive and their orientation becomes more problem-solving focused than vision creating.In fact, in most organisations more energy is used for fixing existing problems than focusing on the mandate and the vision of the organisation.

Real Change Must Start with Engaging Every Employee at the Core

The only way to keep teams focused on your organisational goals during times of change is to create a culture where every individual feels in their very core that focusing on the highest aspirations and meaningful goals of the company is more important than the uncomfortable feelings created by change.

Chapter 6

6. Three Steps to Building a Sustainable High Performance Organisation

A key ingredient to transforming your business from the status quo to a sustainable, high performance organisation, therefore, is your corporate culture. When you build a corporate culture of excellence, you create organisational capacity and a structure that empowers, focuses and engages employees. You stop nurturing an outmoded culture focused on problem-solving. Instead, you expend your energy and resources to equip your teams with the right mindset and skills necessary to focus on creating the desired results.

A dysfunctional culture can drive your best talent away; an exciting, supportive, and empowering one can attract and retain them.

As an organisation, you also need to help employees develop the flexibility and resilience to deal with change, challenge and uncertainty that may arise along the way. This will ensure that they are ready to learn, absorb and retain new skills and stay focused on their goals.

Finally, your leaders need to embrace practical coaching for excellence skills to sustain your momentum over the long term. Without this internal leadership and coaching capacity in place you will resort to the old pattern of finding short term solutions that fall by the wayside as employees slip back to their old habits.

By implementing a three-phase process, you can start building a new culture of excellence and creating an organisation where your employees feel empowered, inspired and motivated.

- Phase 1: Mindset of Excellence. The first step to building a corporate culture that will drive a high performance organisation is to create a mindset that will engage and align every employee with your vision, mission and values, and leave them speaking a common language of excellence. You will build a new capacity for growth. Your employees will think in more creative and innovative ways, and will develop the tolerance to continue to move forward despite challenges, change and potential distractions.

- Phase 2: Strategies for Excellence. With the new mindset of excellence in place, your teams will be ready to focus on achieving their specific goals and plans for performance excellence. This phase is all about growth—building the skills and competencies required to grow the business.
- Phase 3: Sustaining Excellence. When the first two phases are complete, you will have a strong collective mindset of excellence in place, alignment around performance goals and the skills and competencies required to deliver excellence. Now, it's time to focus on developing strong leadership to ensure that the new mindset and performance skills learned are sustainable and simply become the way things are done. This is a critical step often missed in organisations — but is required to ensure that employees don't revert back to old habits.

Chapter 7

7. Building a Culture of Excellence Organisation- Wide

Some companies make the mistake of limiting their corporate culture development to just their leadership or executive team, and hope it will simply trickle down to the rest of the organisation. Or they may think they have a revenue problem or a customer service prob-lem, and limit their focus to specific teams.

While there are times that high performance companies experience particular issues related to a single team, the most successful companies focus on building a culture of excellence organisation-wide. They understand that every part of the organisation has an impact on the other parts, and that the most powerful results are created when every part is in sync.

By focusing on every employee and team across the organisation, you will ensure that each individual:

• Is aligned to a common vision that is inspiring and meaningful, a vision that
The entire organisation is proud to work toward.
• Understands what the end goal is, where the company is now and, specifi-cally, how to bridge the gap between the two.

Leadership Excellence

If your executives and leaders don't have the right mindset in place, no amount of leader-ship development and skills training will ever make a difference because distractions due to feelings of powerlessness, insecurity, avoidance, resentment, fear of change, or a pro-a tectionist mentality will prevent them from being fully open, interested and curious about the new learning.

However, if you focus on building the appropriate leadership culture and mindset first, fears, resentment and confidence issues will be transformed into opportunities for growth, greater team cohesion and collaboration and a leadership team that is engaged and ready to learn.

When your leaders have the right outlook and truly apply practical leadership and coaching skills, not only do team members feel encouraged and supported, but they know that their roles and work matter, which results in higher levels of motivation and independence to work toward their goals. This frees up leaders and managers to move away from problem-solving and baby-sitting, and focus instead on what they are supposed to do, be strategic and improve team performance.

Leadership doesn't just happen. But when it's done right, the result is highly committed and engaged teams, with high levels of communication, workflow and productivity.

Sales Excellence

While it's common knowledge that a high performance sales team is vital to the financial success of any organisation, many companies simply go from one sales training program to another, getting the same results each time—short term rises in performance and productivity that quickly drop off as sales people drift back to their old habits and routines.

Once again, if your sales people don't have the right mindset in place, no amount of skills training will ever make a difference. Your sales team may lack assertiveness, commitment or focus but if you first concentrate on building the right sales culture and mindset, fears of rejection and confidence problems go away. Your sales team will become more confident, assertive,
receptive and accountable—and will be able to deal with the different challenges facing them.

Teams that have achieved sales excellence operate from a customer mindset. They understand the needs and motivations of customers and partner with them to create a result that is mutually beneficial to both parties. It is all about relationships and partnership.

Customer Service Excellence
The essence of customer service excellence is the ability to create a memorable and positive experience. This experience must be unique to your organisation and consistent at every touch

point, whether it's on the phone with a representative, in person at the front desk, or speaking with the accounting department.

In order to deliver this level of customer service, a mindset or culture of excellence is again required. Only then will your customer service teams understand that a great service experience is not created simply through applying some skills, but comes from the energy and core essence of each person.

Service excellence is the ability to create a connection with the customer so that they feel you genuinely care about the fulfilment of their needs. This generates the superior service experience that causes them to come back for more. It creates the buzz and reference base that every company wants.

Team Excellence

If companies do not have that unifying element that comes from a strong corporate and team culture, most people will be more focused on protecting their own agenda rather than working collaboratively with others in a spirit of openness and common interest.

In order to create team excellence, there has to be a common unifying goal and aspira-tion that brings people together—where everyone on the team understands that by working together as a team, everyone will benefit more: individually, as a team, as an organisation, and with customers.

To truly achieve team excellence, each individual must believe that by working together they will achieve more than by protecting their knowledge, skills and expertise.

Operational Excellence

To achieve operational excellence in a manufacturing environment, every team member has to have the right mindset in place, and understand the specific goals they are working toward. These goals must be motivating, inspiring, and ones that can only be reached by working together.

With the right outlook, skills and coaching in place, operational teams work in the same ways that the very top sport teams operate. They are not focused on beating the other team but rather on beating the clock, breaking records, and achieving something that has not been achieved before. On the production line, this creates excitement, energy and positive tensions.

Chapter 8

8. Sustaining Excellence: Don't Settle for Short-Term Results

Don't send your staff and leaders to skills training alone. While you may see some initial short-term results, they will drop off as your employees fall back into their old habits. You need to have a plan in place to ensure that all the work you've done on your corporate culture, engaging your employees and giving them strategies for success is sustainable over the long term.

A key ingredient to sustaining excellence is equipping your managers with leadership and coaching for excellence skills. Once your leaders have become competent at using these different skills to improve the performance of their teams, they will be able to:

• Remove any distractions that could be getting in the way of maximising performance.

- Effectively coach their team members to un-tap their potential.
- Motivate and improve the confidence of their team members.
- Increase the focus and performance of their team.
- Increase their team's resilience and ability to deal with change and uncertainty.
- Enhance the creativity and innovation of their team members.
- Deliver excellence with their teams.
- Sustain your momentum over the long term.

Your leaders' focus will move from solving small problems, to coaching, leading and motivating their teams to stay aligned with the goals and vision of the company and move the business forward toward excellence.

Chapter 9

Does Your Company Need a Corporate Culture Health Check?

Often, it's the companies that are already doing really well that realise what an impact corporate culture has on their organisations. These companies invest continually in improving their corporate cultures to support growth.

For most companies, however, there is a significant event or trigger that causes them to seek help. These triggers include:
- Mergers and acquisitions
- Moving from a private to a public company
- Privatisation of a government or crown-type corporation
- Restructuring or new leadership
- Industry changes and increased competition
- Any significant change, including rapid growth.

Symptoms That Indicate You May Have a Corporate Culture Challenge

There are a few telling symptoms that show that your company has a corporate culture challenge:

1. *Distractions*: Your employees are distracted, and your managers are spending a lot of time dealing with small issues and problems when they should be focusing on your vision and goals.

2. *Silos and Conflict*: People are not working well together, and each department is guarding its own turf instead of working towards the common goals.

3. *Arrogance and Egos*: There are a lot of egos strutting around believing they already
know it all and are above everyone else. This indicates that people are closed off and aren't open to hearing ideas and suggestions that might be better than their own and that could improve the business.

4. *Lack of Accountability*: Your employees are not taking full responsibility for their goals and their role in the company. Instead of focusing on improvement, they make excuses for poor performance and incomplete assignments, and lament that they aren't paid enough.

If any of the above scenarios sound familiar, you could have a corporate culture that is
stuck on problem-solving versus vision creating. These are two hugely different focuses—the one delivers excellence and the other wastes your time and resources.

A Quick Quiz to determine if you have a Culture of Excellence

Culture of excellence health check

To what extent do you agree or disagree with each of the statement below	1.	2.	3.	4.	5.
1. The company has the mindset and culture to respond quickly to external changes.					
2. We are all working towards the same end goal – pulling in the same direction (rather than working in silos)					
3. As employees we are encouraged to challenge the status quo in order to optimise everything we do					
4. We have the mindset and resilience to face challenges head on and deal with them					
5. Our organisation focuses as much on achieving business results as it does on people engagement					
6. Our organisation ensures that all leaders (particularly the CEO and Senior Leadership Team) base their actions on rock solid values, without compromise.					

The numbers on the table represents the following:
1. *Strongly disagree*
2. *Disagree*

3. Neither agree nor disagree
4. Agree
5. Strongly agree

If you rated your organisation less than 4 (average), it is most likely that there is a gap between the culture you are aspiring for and the culture you currently have.

Building a Culture of Excellence will enable you to attract and hire the best people, increase engagement amongst your current people, and improve your overall performance and profitability.

Chapter 10

UNDERSTANDING HOW ORGANISED STRUCTURE BUILDS CULTURE OF EXCELLENCE

Large enterprises require an established, organised structure to coordinate large numbers of employees and avoid chaos. But smaller businesses and startups rarely think of designing an organisational structure in the first place

What Is Organisational Structure?
Organisational structure is the backbone of all the operating procedures and workflows at any company. It determines the place and the role of each employee in the business, and is key to organisational development.

A clear structure allows every team member to be involved. When employees know what they're responsible for and who they report to – which isn't the case in many fast-growing companies – they're more likely to take ownership of their work.

To build an organisation structure, you need to consider your business size, life cycle, goals, and positioning. Apart from considering the current environment your company operates in, you should also think of where you want to see the organisation in five years – as its a pillar of organisational health.

Is It Possible to Change an Organisation's Structure?

Of course, organisational design can be reconstructed if needed. The business landscape is constantly evolving, and keeping to a structure that has worked for years might simply become inefficient.

To adapt to market changes, you might need to resort to organisational transformation which affects not only your strategy but also the structure. Whether you want to build an organisational structure from scratch or want to revisit the existing one, you'll need to get down to the basics.

An organisational structure is based on a range of elements, including:

- Work specialisation
- Departmentation
- Chain of command
- Span of control

- Centralization/Decentralisation
- Formalisation

Work specialisation
Work specialisations define how responsibilities are split between employees based on the job description. It's used to split projects into smaller work activities and assign digestible tasks to individual employees. The most common results of improper specialisation are low efficiency and burnout.

Documentation
Documentation is an act of grouping specialists on the basis of the job description, skills, location, or other factors that connect them.

The biggest challenge is choosing the criteria for departmentation. In many cases, it's no more enough to apply functional departmentation – where employees are grouped based on the tasks they perform. Startups often go for matrix departmentation that involves combining two types of departmentation and takes the best out of both worlds. For instance, functional departmentation can be joined by geographical departmentation to better serve clients in different locations.

Chain of command

Chain of command represents a system for passing instructions and reporting within an organisation. Ideally, it distributes the power, supports knowledge sharing, and encourages employee accountability.

The traditional chain of command makes decision-making more complex and does not allow for much flexibility. On the contrary, modern approaches strive to enhance employee autonomy and avoid micromanagement.

Span of control

Span of control regulates the number of direct reporters managed by a single supervisor. It heavily depends on the three aforementioned elements of organisational structure. Furthermore, to identify the right span of control, you need to evaluate your leaders' capacity, workplace size, and experience level of employees.

Centralization and decentralisation
Centralization and decentralisation are the concepts defining how managers, as well as employees, give input on company goals and strategy. While centralization gives leaders the ultimate control over decision-making processes, decentralisation allows employees to impact business decisions. We'll dive into centralised and decentralised organisational structures in the further section.

Formalisation
Formalisation determines to which extent business processes, policies, and job descriptions are standardised. It may regulate communication between employees and managers, workplace culture, operational procedures, etc.

Centralised vs. Decentralised Organisational Structures
Back to centralization and decentralisation. When designing an organisational structure, you'll need to choose a side. Do you want to

implement top-down or bottom-up management?

Centralised organisational structure
As has been said, in a centralised organisational structure, decisions are made by top managers and are distributed down the chain of command.

For sure, the structure has a range of advantages. It ensures greater control over business processes. But most importantly, it only includes highly experienced professionals that are able to foresee the effect of decisions made in the long run.

centralised-org-structure
The biggest drawback of a centralised organisational structure is the amount of time the decision-making process takes in large companies. Imagine a customer support manager being asked to implement an exclusive package for a high-ticket customer. To get permission, they'd need to run the request up the chain of command and wait for it to be processed by top management. When the

request is approved, a high-ticket customer might no longer be there.

Decentralised organisational structure
To avoid this issue, large organisations turn to decentralisation. In a decentralised structure, lower-level employees pinpoint issues and make decisions before communicating it to upper management. Greater autonomy not only empowers employees but also eliminates process delays, which are common for centralised systems.
decentralised-org-structure
However, decentralisation also brings coordination challenges and higher expenses.

Often, it's recommended that early-stage startups and small businesses go after a centralised organisational structure. Fast-growing companies and enterprises usually choose a decentralisation framework.

Chapter 11

7 Types of Organisational Structures

The key purpose of any organisational structure is to make the processes more straightforward. However, there are many ways to achieve that.

Let's look into the seven types of organisational structure and pick the one that will strengthen your company.

1. Functional structure

A functional structure groups employees into different departments by work specialisation. Each department has a designated leader highly experienced in the job functions of each employee supervised by them.

Most often, it implements a top-down (centralised) decision-making process where department managers report to upper management. Ideally, leaders of different teams communicate regularly and coordinate their strategies while lower-level employees have little idea of the processes taking place outside their department.

The main challenge companies with a functional structure face is the lack of coordination between departments. Employees may lose the larger company context when focusing on very specific tasks and failing to interact with members of other departments.

To create a functional organisational structure that works, you'll need to train leaders to foster collaboration across departments

2. Divisional structure

A divisional structure organises employees around a common product or geographical location. Divisional organisations have teams focused on a specific market or product line.

Examples of companies applying a divisional structure are McDonald's Corporation and Disney. These brands can't help but split the entire organisation by location to be able to adjust their strategies for audiences representing different markets.

These smaller groups are relatively independent and mainly follow a decentralised framework. Still, the leaders of each department are likely to operate under centralised corporate management. It means that company culture is dictated by top management, but operational decisions can be made by each division independently.

Giants such as McDonald's and Disney also add functional units to their structure for better control.

3. Matrix structure
Within a matrix organisational structure, team members report to several managers at once. Wait, what's the point?

Having multiple supervisors allows for company-wide interaction and faster project delivery. For instance, when answering to functional managers and project managers, employees have a chance to collect experience outside their team. While functional managers can help to solve job-specific issues, project managers can bring in knowledge or talents from other departments.

matrix-structure-example
If you go after a matrix organisational structure, you'll need to find a way to avoid authority confusion and prevent conflicts between managers.

4. Team structure
A team-based organisational structure creates small teams that focus on delivering one product or service. These teams are capable of solving problems and making decisions without bringing in third parties.

team-structure-example
Team members are responsible for managing their workload and have full control over the project. Team-based organisations are distinguished by little formalisation and high flexibility. This structure works well for global organisations and manufacturers.

5. Network structure

A network structure goes far beyond your internal company structure. It's an act of joining the efforts of two or more organisations with the goal of delivering one product or service. Typically, a network organisation outsources independent contractors or vendors to complete the work.

network-approach-to-structure
In a network organisation, teams are built from full-time employees as well as freelance specialists – this way, in-house workers can spend most of their time focusing on the work they specialise in. Such an approach allows companies to adapt to market changes and obtain the missing skills fast.

Working with individuals that aren't integrated into your company culture results in lower formalisation and higher agility.

6. Hierarchical structure

You must already have an idea of what a hierarchical structure is. It's the most common organisational structure type that follows a direct chain of command.

A chain of command, in this case, goes from senior management to general employees through a range of executives on the departmental and team level. The highest-level executive has the highest power over the decision-making process.

hierarchical structure chart example
On one hand, this structure enables organisations to streamline business processes, develop clear career paths, and reduce conflicts. A company hierarchy leaves no place for challenging managers' authority, which can be good in some cases.

On the other hand, a hierarchical structure slows down decision-making and may hurt employee morale.

7. Flat organisation structure

In a flat organisational structure, there are few middle managers between employees and top managers. The structure requires less supervision, increases employee involvement, and boosts trust in the workplace.

flat-organisational-structure-example
Due to its simple nature, a flat organisation structure, also called a "flatarchy", is typically used by small businesses and startups.

Chapter 12

How to Design Your Organisation's Structure

Whatever structure you choose, you'll need to make an effort to implement it. Here are eight simple steps towards designing an organisational structure from scratch.

1. Create a charter
First of all, you need to prepare documentation.

You need a project charter outlining the purpose of building a clear structure, key stakeholders, and their responsibilities. This is your rough plan for implementing an organisational structure that should give you a direction for your next steps.

When creating a charter, you'll be able to answer the following questions:

Why do we need to design (or re-design) an organisational structure?
When do we start?
Who are the key stakeholders in this project?

What should we do first?
Where is the company headed? Will our organisational structure be relevant in a year?

2. Build your strategy

To build a structure from scratch, you'll need to start by outlining a long-term strategy and mapping out goals. Your future vision of your company determines which type of organisational structure will work best for you.

3. Assess your internal processes & systems

If your business has already been operating for quite some time, take a look at your current strategy and try to highlight the areas of improvement. Do you need to revisit your core ideology and company culture? You can only answer this question by talking to your employees and managers.

When you know where you stand and have a clear vision of what you want to achieve, creating an organisational direction shouldn't be a problem.

4. Design your structure

A clear understanding of your company's strategy lets you filter out irrelevant organisational structure types and pick the one that fits with your core values, mission, and goals.

Choose one of the seven organisational structures and use it as a template for designing a custom organisational chart. This chart is also known as an organogram – it's a diagram used to visualise the relationships between individuals, teams, and departments within an organisation

5. *Create a transition plan*
Next, it's time to design an optimal workflow for implementing or switching to a new structure.

Talk to the stakeholders and decide on the deadlines for establishing a brand new organisational structure. Prepare a list of recommendations for top managers and team leaders that will help to communicate the change to the rest of the organisation.

6. *Implement your new structure*

From there, leaders should create an implementation plan that includes training their teams to adopt new roles and skills, as well as how to follow a new decision-making and reporting framework. Week by week, employees will become accustomed to their new organisational structure and adapt to the change.

7. *Monitor the impact*

The transition process might take months, and it's very likely that the performance of individual employees or even entire teams will go down at some point. However, you can assess the impact of a new structure in action only after the transition is complete.

With a new organisational structure in place, run the performance review and talk to executives. It's important that you monitor the contribution of each individual department – chances are the changes don't work equally well for everyone at the company.

8. Gather feedback & improve

Again, once you implement an organisational structure, it's never too late to make adjustments. Alongside performance checks, survey your employees to learn how they feel about a new structure. It can be that their input will help you fine-tune the organisational design without extra cost and effort.

www.ingramcontent.com/pod-product-compliance
Lightning Source LLC
Chambersburg PA
CBHW050312220526
45465CB00005B/1949